All Revolutionary Q's

Proposes

Revolution for Black Fraternity Relevance to the
Global African Struggle

Table of Contents

Preface

ALL Revolutionary Qs (ALLRQs) Message to the Community

Greetings to our Loving and Supporting Community,

We are eternally grateful for your consistent uplift through our collective struggle for peace, justice and liberation. We remain in debt to you for your love and support. As we are all servants of the Creator, we thank you for lifting us to leadership and we realize that we must serve on a higher level. Therefore, we hold ourselves accountable to the Creator and you.

As you have uplifted us, we will strive to uplift you by scientifically examining our collective condition and utilizing our resources to improve our collective condition.

Our founding fathers established a national college fraternity of black men in 1911. At that time, their ages ranged from 20-28 years of age which would amount to them being born between the years 1883-1891. That means that they reached an academic level of attending college as possibly the first generation liberated from the chattel slave system that made it illegal for them to even learn to read. By 1911 one of our founding fathers had reached a level of graduate education in cytology (cell science) and was excelling beyond the formal slave owners with ground breaking scientific discovery. That is a testament of what we can achieve today if we collectively and scientifically analyze our condition and utilize our abilities to improve our condition.

In our commitment and rededication to you, we must apologize for getting side tracked by the good times of prosperity that your uplift provided. We apologize for exploiting and misappropriating the resources that your uplift allowed us to acquire. We apologize for relishing in our physical prowess with hedonistic quest and conquest. We apologize for disrespecting you at times with bravado and the misogyny we learned from the enemies of our community. Along with these apologies, ALL R Qs offers atonement and a recommitment of love, respect, admiration and appreciation for you.

All R Qs humbly seeks to serve you and all that we ask from you is, "How can we better serve you for the next one hundred years and beyond?"

We hope that the ideas presented in this book will provide ideas that will inspire the collective work and responsibility that it will take for systematic impact on uplifting our global community while identifying and eliminating the impediments to that objective.

Chapter 1

New Narrative in the next page of Omega History

As you look at the smiling faces of our Founders and read our fraternity history, it is apparent that we have been a fun loving group of brothers from the birth of our fraternity and that has lived on for now 104 years. Our motto is "Friendship is Essential to the Soul", and within that motto it is clear that the happiness and wellbeing of our souls is at least partially dependent on Friendships. Our fraternity also prides itself on achieving the scholarship to ignite the flaming light of knowledge. It is that light that shines on introspection and contemplation of the global condition of our friends. The light of introspection allows us to see that our motto of friendship is not limited to friendships within our fraternity and that we must truly be friends of the world which connects our souls to all life. Therefore, coupled with the joy that our friends bring to our soul, we also have much pain in our soul as we witness the conditions of friends globally. As we witness the systemic global assault on our people/friends, the Omega lamp should be burning even brighter in our hearts and minds as we contemplate transformative solutions to uplift our people/friends. It is the love of our people/friends that provides the muse for the following words of which I humbly request that we consider. The history of Omega did not end with Brother Herman Dreer's book "The History of Omega Psi Phi Fraternity", published in 1940, nor did the need for a concerted effort toward the global uplift of our people. Therefore, we must write a new narrative and develop a new strategy to ensure advancement for our friends in the 21st century.

Omega Psi Phi Fraternity, Inc.'s constitution and by-laws states its main purpose as follows:

- To bring about a union of college men of similar high ideals of scholarship and manhood in order to occupy a progressive, helpful and constructive place in the civic and political life domestically and internationally; Omega is to prepare its members for greater usefulness in causes of humanity, freedom, and dignity of the individual. Lastly, it is to aid down-trodden humanity in its effort to achieve higher social, economic and intellectual status.

That is a powerful purpose that clearly indicates that our mission is to be a friend of the world and to collectively uphold our global responsibility for uplift. However, Omega has not initiated any national or international strategy to collectively uphold this global responsibility in a substantive way. Therefore, Omega must comprehensively analyze the systemic etiology of the global exploitation and assault on the poor and oppressed people of the world with a particular focus on African people as we are predominantly comprised of men of African descent and Africans have arguably been the most oppressed people on the planet. This analysis is necessary for Omega to organize a comprehensive program that can bring the aforementioned stated purpose of Omega to fruition.

Certainly, the humanity, freedom and dignity of our people has been consistently threaten. Recently, due to progressive non-commercially sponsored media, cell phone video technology as well as social media, we have been able to expose enough of these threats to more vividly illustrate the historically persistent infringement upon our dignity, humanity and freedom by the corporate elite and state sponsored extrajudicial enforcement officers. The news publication entitled, "The Guardian", continues to post what they call "The Count" which provides a "real time" account of the number of murders by the police. (Keep in mind that this report would not include cases like Sandra Bland, Trayvon Martin, the Charleston, S.C. church massacre or the unnamed 14 year old black girl that was physically and in some ways sexually abused by a white McKinney, Texas police officer on camera for the whole world to see.) However, it does show the grossly disproportionate number of Africans being killed by police in America. It notes that in 2015 there have been 2.08 per million whites killed by police compared to 2.33 per million Latinos and 5.19 per million blacks. It seems like daily the media is reporting the horrifying last cries of anguish as we are brutalized and murdered. The last cries have left indelible scars on our hearts and they permanently resonate in minds. You hear them, right? Perhaps the word collage created below will refresh your memory

– "I can't breathe", "Hands up Don't Shoot", "I am innocent", "It was a cell phone", "Call my Mama", "She was only 14" , "Can't we Just all get along", "Don't do this", "Should driving with a damaged tail light lead to death by law?" "I didn't even do nothing", "Why am I being arrested?" "Black Lives Matter", "He was only 12", "He had on a hoody and his Ice Tea looked Dangerous", "Haitian voices cry as they are murdered by U.S. backed puppet regimes of Haiti and the Dominican Republic", "Millions of last cries by Congolese killed by U.S. supported proxy wars", "African immigrants fleeing Libya due to the U.S. dismantling of that sovereign state", "Little Boys of the Central African Republic scream in terror as they are raped by U.N. so called Peace Keeping forces", "West Papuan cries from murder by U.S. backed Indonesian troops" "Palestinian cries within the Apartheid state created by U.S. backed Israeli forces", "Mexican/Latin American and Central American Immigrants cries due to U.S. backed militias and economic policies imposed on their governments ", "The 99% cries for economic justice" "The Mass Incarcerated cry for justice", "Political Prisoners cry for justice" and the Earth screams as it is ravaged environmentally by misguided capitalists' interest..... –

These haunting cries add clarity as to what our mission for uplift must be. As Omega is a predominately African/black fraternity, its very existence is threaten by the systematic destruction of black men and the women that produce those men. It is clear that saving our people is synonymous with preserving our fraternity. In order to broach the noble yet monumental task of saving our people we must consider some our current global conditions:

- Omega must be cognizant of the systematic criminalization of fatherhood through inequitable family court systems that are completely insensitive to paternal needs of the black family and extremely bias against fathers.
- Omega must see that our often innocent fathers, uncles, brothers, cousins, friends are harassed, assaulted and murdered by extrajudicial enforcement officers.
- Omega has to be "Fired Up" as we witness our often innocent women and little girls tackled and shackled by state sponsored enforcement officers just as we were manacled and shackled upon arriving to this land in 1619.
- Omega must be charged to utilize its intellectual pool to challenge the judicial system that is allowing these atrocities to occur with impunity.
- Omega must be charged in utilizing its intellectual pool and financial resources to address the fact that 39% of African children in the U.S. live below the poverty line.
- Omega must utilizes its intellectual pool of African men to address the economic conditions that place our people at risks socially, medically, politically, educationally and financially.
- Omega must see that the recent incidents in Charleston, S.C. demonstrates that a white supremacist system is educating its youth as well as the general public to support global white supremacist ideology for the sake of world domination. So clearly Omega must pool its professional educators to counter that miseducation in order to develop a more pluralistic and egalitarian society.
- Omega must understand the global implications of our tax dollars being spent on the U.S. military's infringement upon the sovereignty and human rights of our people in Africa and the African Diaspora
- Omega must consider organizing itself as a self-sustaining movement that constructively merges the necessary politics

of protest with electoral politics while integrating and engaging with international governing bodies for support.

- Omega must be charged in addressing the disparities that cause our people to be disproportionately impoverished, imprisoned, under/unemployed, miseducated, malnourished and in poorer health as a whole.
- Omega must be charged with addressing the moral decadence and cultural bankruptcy our people are experiencing through mass media propaganda, miseducation and destruction of our family/community unit.

If Omega can address these matters and more, it will most certainly fulfill its purpose of occupying a progressive, helpful and constructive place in the civic and political life of its people domestically and internationally.

In order to demonstrate why a systematic effort will be necessary to counter state sponsored terror on Omega's people, a succinct overview of the systematic effort to oppress African people has been described below.

History well documents that since the advent of chattel-slavery, African people have been the prey of white supremacist's financial interest. The white supremacists knew that a strong people would not continue to be enslaved voluntarily, so in their sick and greedy desire to control and exploit, they developed a comprehensive system of brutality. That system of brutality was state sponsored then and it remains state sponsored now resulting in the brutal social conditions Africans face today. Additionally, after chattel-slavery ended, African people had been rendered dependent upon ex-slave masters because they had virtually no means of self-sustaining production; limited land and limited equipment for development/cultivation/irrigation of the land; and no self-sustaining economic, educational, vocational, medical or governmental infrastructure. Therefore, they had limited means of establishing their own basic housing, enterprises or institutions of development. Additionally, the white supremacist ruling class feared Africans that were once brutally enslaved would rise up and seek violent retribution as they had rightfully done on numerous occasion during slavery. Consequently, the white supremacist ruling class deemed Africans as expendable surplus labor that needed to be depopulated. Therefore, white supremacist began to develop systems of imprisonment and extermination via anti-loitering acts, false charges leading to rampant false imprisonment, and pervasive lynching. Again, remnants of that system remains today. That system has produced colonization and undermining of sovereign African states as well as state sponsored distribution of illicit and highly addictive narcotics within various predominately African communities in America and abroad. Additionally, it has contributed to environmental racism, murder and mass incarceration of African people.

As stated at the 2015 Social Forum in NYC, NY, as white supremacists have developed a global capitalist structure, they have commodified everything, including people. Based on that commodification of people, they find many Africans of lower economic status to be more valuable - for capitalist interest - in prison than being free. The rationale of that social theory postulates that if their wages are low they pay minimal to no taxes and may also need supplemental government services that cost the government money. However, if we are imprisoned, we (as an African people) can be exploited for practically free labor for prison industry production to consequently build the prison industry which is now publically trading on the U.S. Stock Exchange. Additionally, the government/state provides subsidies to the prison system to maintain Africans and other downtrodden people in a white supremacist system with stark similarities to slavery. As a matter of fact, the U.S. Constitution's 13th Amendment clearly states, "Neither slavery nor involuntary servitude, **except as a punishment for crime whereof the party shall have been duly convicted, shall exist within the United States**, or any place subject to their jurisdiction." Clearly the mass incarceration of Africans here in America work to re-establish slavery under a different name.

During the Left Forum Conference in N.Y.C., 2014, Glen Ford (editor, journalist, broadcaster and activist) noted that land is commodified in urban areas where many Africans reside and the brutal extrajudicial system works to eliminate and displace them in order to gentrify the land for corporate interest. He noted that as urban renewal politicians and investors displace and depopulate black people, they can revalue the land and property at a higher rate. He noted that this is because white supremacists corporate elite place a lower land and property value on places inhabited by Africans. That social theory appears to play out in various urban areas within the United States and abroad.

In order to depopulate the down-trodden, African people in the urban areas of the United States are being terrorized by state sponsored white supremacist extrajudicial enforcement agencies. The terrorism includes harassment; predatory legal policies, citations, laws, fees and penalties creating debtors prisons; brutality including state sponsored illegal interrogation centers; state sponsored murder resulting in no or minimal penalties for the extrajudicial enforcers. Additionally, African people are often falsely convicted of crimes and falsely imprisoned as well as entrapped.

That was some historical context to briefly explain the global systemic actions that create downtrodden humanity. It is important that we understand the root causes in order to develop a collective strategy to root them out.

The thoughts below present ideas as to how Omega can be relevant to the struggle of our people:

Our courageous youth are challenging the state sponsored terror on African people through uprisings, civil disobedience and other creative expressions of warranted outrage. They have not ceased even after the media sensationalism has left. However, these necessary acts of courage need funding and other support to sustain themselves. Protest politics need funding for supplies, bail for protesters, lawyers, food, shelter and even income streams to sustain the protest. Protest politics can set the climate for electoral politics if strategically planned and they are vital to the transformative change necessary. Omega cannot only help this movement but launch a paralleled economic movement for self-determination with necessary international implications. This movement will be explained in the chapter entitled, "From Bricks to BRICS"

As this book explores how Omega can become relevant to the struggle of African people through economic empowerment. We must consider that Omega is in a unique position to economically and intellectually support a national/international movement to uplift African people who are a large part of the downtrodden. Omega is in this unique position because it has an economic infrastructure that generates capital without the external support of other people seeking to alter the agenda to serve interest external to the agenda. Omega also has the intellectual capital capable of implementing economic, social, educational and cultural programs that can systematically uplift the down trodden in a substantive way.

Omega is in this unique position because it is a non-profit incorporation with a commercial brand that is marketed and sold.

The brand has successfully sold for 104 years and it has produced other products and ways of producing revenue. It also has its own banking system with the strong potential for expansion. If Omega's system can efficiently be used to build educational, political, social and cultural programs to uplift African people, it will in turn uplift humanity. This is because if you can uplift the most oppressed people of the world, all of the world should invariably be uplifted as well.

The purpose of this book is to inspire us to continue to fulfill our purpose in the context of today's challenges and to spell out practical strategies for us to consider implementing collectively as an international agenda.

Chapter 2

From Bricks to BRICS – A New Economic Structure is under Construction

In Omega Psi Phi Fraternity, it is sometimes a ritualistic practice to carry bricks a part of an extremely challenging process of entering Omega. Carrying the brick is a symbolic embodiment of the organization and how it must continually be built, protected, and how its members must perpetually build for others as they strive to climb. Omega has a Federal Credit Union called, Omega Psi Phi Federal Credit Union (OPPFCU). The credit union was established by forward thinking brothers like the late Brother James A. Elam. Against all odds, Brother Elam and other dedicated Omega men, established OPPFCU as the first Credit Union based on a fraternal organization. OPPFCU is one of only two active Credit Unions in the world chartered by the National Credit Union Administration (NCUA) as a fraternal associational organization. That was a monumental achievement for self-determination that must be advanced to meet today's economic challenges facing our brothers and our people.

Omega Psi Phi Fraternity Inc., currently has several sources of revenue from membership dues, initiation fees, chapter dues, international meetings, national/local meetings, registration fees, paraphernalia, merchandise, entertainment, etc. However, Omega invests the majority of its revenue into Commercial Banks and a negligible amount of it into its own credit union with no investments into its Credit Union on a consistent uniformed basis. Therefore, it contributes to the growth of the "Corporate elite" and a Finance Capitalist system that works to the demise of its people while contributing minimally to the development of itself or the people of which its founders intended to uplift.

Therefore, in an effort to make Omega more relevant to the global African struggle and the struggle of oppressed people in general, a few courageous and forward thinking brothers of Omega Psi Phi Fraternity drafted a recommendation to Omega's Conclave requesting that Omega divest from all commercial banks and into its own credit union. The Omega International Conclave was held on the week of July 13-17, 2014. (As you read further, you will see that this was a historically significant week for not only black self-determination, but self-determination of developing nations globally). During that Conclave, a movement for black self-determination was initiated by the aforementioned recommendation. The purpose of the initiative was to build wealth to strengthen the Black community through building its own economy independent of the commercial banking system. This movement was met with silent resistance from intra-fraternal leadership and subterfuge efforts to silence the movement. During the Conclave, the Grand Basileus autocratically altered the Conclave Plenary Session agenda so that the voting delegates as well as other attendees would not be informed of the Divestment Recommendation let alone vote on it. After there was a complaint filed, the Leadership rounded up a few delegates - two days after the recommendation was up for an official vote - in order to vote on the recommendation without quorum and without presenting the information explaining the recommendation to the general body of brothers in attendance at the Conclave. That subterfuge act was not only an affront on Omega's democratic process but it betrayed the very purpose of our fraternity. That purpose being as follows:

- To bring about a union of college men of similar high ideas of scholarship and manhood in order to occupy a progressive, helpful and constructive place in the civic and political life domestically and internationally; Omega is to prepare its members for greater usefulness in causes of humanity, freedom, and dignity of the individual. Lastly, it is to aid down-trodden humanity in its effort to achieve higher social, economic and intellectual status.

Divestment from Commercial Banks and Investment into OPPFCU would strengthen Omega's financial position nationally and internationally which would strengthen its philanthropy in order to uplift black people who are suffering from austerity measures initiated by the corporate elites' control over government policies geared to propagate free market capitalism.
Investment of revenue into OPPFCU would increase Omega's liquid capital and increase its lending power for its people. It would also allow Omega to be a major contributor to mass cooperative economics programs to uplift oppressed people. It would also pay dividends to its members and lead to more transparency in accounting because all members would have access to earnings reports.

Managed properly, the increased financial strength of Omega could lead to - but not limited to - the following for Omega:

- The building of trade schools to teach our youth skills that would enable them to establish meaningful businesses and gain meaningful employment rather than hopelessness and self-destruction;
- The building of social programs e.g. Houses of Literacy leading to higher geopolitical awareness and Mathematical Literacy, Life Skills, Rehabilitation centers, Recreation Centers; African Cultural/Art Centers;
- The ability to provide more substantial academic and trade school scholarships;
- The building of community health centers/hospitals;
- The building of strong financial lending institutions for homes, autos and business.

There are endless possibilities and this could be our divine destiny to forward our struggle.

Omega has a golden opportunity to be the next major movement for black people if it seizes the time to be the first black "so called" Greek organization to utilize its resources to build an economy to be utilized for the uplift of Black people. That would certainly be a living example of what Omega men carry Bricks for during the ritualistic process.

To draw the relevant international parallel, during the same week of July 13-17, 2014, on the world stage global BRICS (an acronym for Brazil, Russia, India, China and South Africa) were also being utilized for global construction of economic self-determination programs for developing nations. The BRICS nations held the 6th BRICS summit in Fortaleza, Brazil. The BRICS - in this case - is an acronym for a group of nations that are the world's largest emerging economies. These nations came together during the summit to sign the long-anticipated document to create the 100 billion dollar BRICS Development Bank and a reserve a currency pool worth over another $100 billion. Both will counter the influence of Western-based lending institutions and the dollar. Documents on cooperation between BRICS export credit agencies and an agreement of cooperation on innovation were also signed. This will have a significant impact on African nations and other developing nations of color being strangled by "loan shark" debts to the World Bank and International Monetary Fund.

This is particularly relevant to Omega's potential banking strategy because if the economic development "Bricks" of Omega could somehow collaborate with the "BRICS" of the Development Bank, it could certainly have an impact on the Western World's financial exploitation over poor and oppressed people of the world if managed in a socialist manner. Thus the title, "From Bricks to BRICS". This could have an impact because instead of African nations paying exorbitant interest rates to former colonial rulers and instead of Omega paying interest to its former enslavers, The BRICS Development Bank could refinance African/African Diaspora nations' debt as well as Omega's loans along with financially backing Omega's Credit portfolio. Consequently, the Omega Credit Union would be empowered to finance loans for the fraternity members and family as well as the black communities nationally in terms of mortgages, auto loans, student loans, personal loans and business loans. Again, Omega could potentially collaborate with the BRICS development bank to have its credit lines backed by BRICS capital as well as refinance current loans OPPFCU and Omega have with Commercial Banks.

On another relevant international note, around the same time as the Omega Conclave and the BRICs development bank meeting, on 11July2014 Russian President Vladimir Putin gave final approval to a measure that wrote off 90 percent of the more than $30 billion in Soviet-era debt Cuba owed Russia. The move came just hours before Putin touched ground in Havana, where he kicked off a six-day tour of Latin America aimed at boosting trade and ties in the region. That move potentially opens another international financial collaboration for Omega if U.S. financial sanctions on Cuba are abolished.

These three events were not directly coordinated but they were indirectly coordinated by default due to persistent oppression, poverty, and displacement of the masses by a corporate elite supported by western imperialist. Historically, oppressed people eventually analyze their condition and develop a strategy to improve their condition. These three correlated events are an example of that historical fact. The additional relevance to all of this in the context of the pervasive extrajudicial and white supremacist brutality black people are facing, organized financial empowerment through international collaboration may be our safest and more effective solution. This will allow Omega to lead black people in providing financial support for protest politics, electoral politics and finance politics. This could be ground breaking and Omega is in a unique position to do it. The next paragraphs will describe the reason why Omega must take on this strategy because finance may be the best and most peaceful option for what we are up against.

In the United States, the corporate elite's strategy to propagate "Free Market Capitalism" by privatizing public institutions and placing a commodity value on everything has taken a devastating toll on the poor and oppressed people because many depend on public programs. Additionally, the masses of people –particularly people of African descent- are devalued and even considered expendable in the commodity market especially if they do not succumb to slave wages.

The common U.S. corporate strategy is to utilize their imperial military might to de-stabilize socialist governments so that they can privatize the natural resources of these socialist nations and exploit the extremely low wage labor market created by displacing people, under educating them and beating them into submission by war, torture, terror and fear. This global imperialist strategy has taken a toll on the working class of America and internationally. The free market policies namely NAFTA (the North Atlantic Free Trade Agreement) – allowed the U.S. and its NATO allies to move companies out of the U.S. to set up in the countries they have destabilized and turned into "client states" to manufacture goods of which were once manufactured by U.S. workers. "Client states" are considered nations that were once sovereign and governed by a republic but are now ruled by neocolonialist leaders that are controlled by imperialist powers.

Due to the limited job and educational opportunities lost to free market capitalism, many poor and oppressed youth of the U.S. choose to serve in the U.S military industrial complex or serve as targets for the U.S. manufactured Global Drug War economy. In both cases, poor and oppressed youth are further exploited. In the military they are brainwashed into risking their lives to fight other poor and oppressed people. They become low wage mercenary killers of oppressed people so that more imperialist companies can move manufacturing, production and mining jobs out of the U.S. and into the conquered counties. This vicious cycle displaces the poor people of those conquered lands and further limits the job opportunities not only for the poor U.S. civilians but also the low wage U.S. soldiers coming home.

In the global U.S. manufactured Drug War, our youth are readily presented with U.S. supported entrapments to sell illegal drugs to potentially improve their poor economic state. Upon falling prey to these entrapments, poor and oppressed youth become targets for U.S. paramilitary and criminal justice landmines that either kill them or feed them to the U.S. Prison Industrial Complex for more corporate profit and ethnic cleansing for the sake of gentrification of urban areas.

Omega Psi Phi Fraternity is a predominately black fraternity and black men are disproportionately affected by this cycle of exploitation. Therefore, as leaders, Omega men must be conscious of this exploitation and carry the symbolic "Brick" to construct a solution. Again, cooperative economics through OPPFCU and BRICS may be part of the solution.

Omega must also be cognizant of the extra layer of systemic racism that compounds the problem. Systemic racism affects the development of black people severely. The effect of systemic racism is very broad and cannot be comprehensively covered in this writing but a few key components will be broached as they pertain to what OPPFCU, BRICS, and opening a relationship with BRICS and possibly Cuba may have the ability to impact:

- On the macro level - economics created in a racist and capitalist system results in an inability for blacks to establish manufacturing facilities; production centers; seaports; rail transportation; airways; construction companies; agricultural facilities; technology & research and development centers; systems of justice; security agencies; institutions of health and medicine; Afrocentric Institutions for Higher Spiritual attainment; Afrocentric educational institutions and financial institutions.
    - o On a micro level - economics created in a racist and capitalist system results in discriminatory hiring; lower wages; unemployment or underemployment;

limited ability to save and invest, limited credit to receive loans as well as predatory lending; inferior training in core curriculum that would prepare students for higher paying careers; substandard living conditions; covert government plots to establish illegal economic opportunities leading to higher crime; police brutality; state sponsored extrajudicial killings; high incarceration rates; medical apartheid, miseducation from a white supremacist public school systems; sub-standard education; and this bleak list can continue.

Some men of Omega Psi Phi are conscious of the aforementioned racist and capitalist assault on black people, some men of Omega feel that it is our duty to strategize to counter that assault of imperialism, capitalism and racism on our people. The founders of Omega noted that our mission is to uplift the downtrodden and our motto is "Friendship is Essential to the Soul". Therefore, we must be a friend to the world by utilizing our resources to foster cooperative economics and self-determination to build a vanguard movement to provide real and substantive uplift for black people. It is our hope that this idea for black self-determination through cooperative economics will spread to other black organizations and grassroots organizations. It is also an aspiration for us to collaborate with the BRICS Movement and the emerging economies of nations such as Cuba or other socialist governments in order to maximize the impact on Imperialist Finance Capital so that new and more equitable governance may emerge.

We must either throw the BRICS/Bricks at Imperialist or Build Counter Institutions with the BRICS/Bricks or both. Either way, we must progress.

Chapter 3

Omega as a Microcosm of the Global Class Struggle

Our Fraternity was established to cultivate friendships to make it easier to navigate through our struggle. Yet, it has become a class based organization that has inevitably entered a class struggle. Within this Class struggle, 3 classes similar to those described by Osagyefo Kwame Nkrumah as well as Karl Marx has posthumously occurred. The 3 delineated classes can be described in terms utilized by the brethren of Omega juxtaposed to terms used by Nkrumah and Marx but indeed there are stark similarities between the classes in whatever way one is inclined to use them. The classes are described as follows:

1. The Omega Elitist Class (Omega Terminology) = Bourgeoisie (Nkrumah/Marx Terminology)

2. The Omega Wannabe Elites (Omega Terminology) = The Petty Bourgeoisie (Nkrumah/Marx Terminology)

3. The Owt Undergraduate/The Ostracized/Expelled/Disenfranchised Revolutionary Class = Proletariat/Workers and Peasants (Nkrumah/Marx Terminology)

Omega Elitist Class (Bourgeoisie) - includes our pseudo wealthy, conservative, reactionary brothers. These brothers consist –largely but not completely- of the brothers that do not take part in a rigorous and lengthy ritualistic rites of passage program known as pledging. However, these brothers typically revere brothers of which they witnessed pledging on their respective campuses (yards) of which they matriculated as undergraduates. The Omega Elitist Class are often professionals, business owners, military officers, high level clergy and a few high level technicians. Within the politics of the fraternity they serve as members of what is known as the Supreme Counsel which includes District Representatives and National Officers. Some serve on the board of directors for companies they set up external to Omega with Omega's funds. They attend fraternal meetings and work within the Elitist Class of the fraternity to maintain the status quo. They control all financial interest in the Fraternity. They are often corrupt and they are mostly all complicit or at least tolerant of the corruption with impunity. In addition to their corruption, they often utilize Omega's resources for their personal gain rather than for the overall uplift of humanity which is noted as Omega's purpose within its constitution. They in turn render Omega irrelevant to the global African struggle.

Omega Wannabe Elites (Petty Bourgeoisie) Class - This class consist of brothers who pledge undergraduate but graduated and joined Graduate Chapters. It also consist of brothers who pledge through a graduate chapter with some pledge practices influenced by the undergraduate pledging practices. These brothers consist of mostly younger "so called" upwardly mobile brothers. These brothers seek to join the Elitist Class and do whatever they feel is necessary to join the Elitist Class. The Elitist Class exploits their desire by using them to monitor and control the Owt Undergrad (Proletariat) Class. The Omega "Wannabe" Elites/Petty Bourgeoisie have limited political power and limited access to fraternity funds but no real intra-fraternal economic power. They serve in political positions such as: Area Representatives for the various national districts, Keepers of Peace, Security and Chaplains. They work to maintain status quo, protect the Elite Class as well as collect the fees charged to the Owt Undergrad Class as well as the Petty Bourgeoisie Class. Just as Nkrumah described the petty bourgeoisie, the roles are similar to tax collectors for the elite and police for the elite.

The Omega Area Representatives are similar to tax collectors and sales representatives for the elitist economic power structure. They travel to various undergraduate chapters of their district and they make sure that undergraduates adhere to financial requirements set by the Elitist Class and attend events that require them to pay fees but provide limited substantive guidance and leadership. An example is what is called, "The Omega Undergraduate Summit". The Elitist Class makes this meeting mandatory for only the Owt Undergraduate/Proletariat Class but they must also pay to attend all the other national meetings held by the Elitist Class. This means that the Class with the most limited income is forced to pay to attend the most meetings and this is enforced by the Area Representatives. During the summit undergraduates are required to be absent from academic class for two to three days and pay for travel to an area convenient for the Elite Class. They also have to pay a fee to register for this meeting were they are trained on how to carry out an Elitist agenda and maintain mandatory fraternity fees. During this meeting, the Elite class never discloses any information regarding the financial status of the fraternity nor does it provide any leadership as to how the Undergraduate/Proletariat Class could use its influence among youth to inspire a substantive youth movement for self-determination. This is very similar to a tax and fee system on the poor and oppressed that yields no representation to influence the tax system or financially benefit from it in any substantive way. However, the Omega Wannabe Elites faithfully works to impose this system on the The Owt Undergrad/ Proletariat Class with aspirations to join the Elite class.

The Owt Undergrad/Proletariat Class - includes brothers that pledged through an undergraduate process. They consist of brothers that go through a challenging ritualistic undergraduate process in order to enter Omega. The process is similar to a rites of passage. They have to be strong bold and courageous to make it through the process and they develop many substantive friendships as the Founders of Omega intended. They are the life blood, enthusiasm, and energy of the fraternity. They attract the energy of young and old people all over the world. They are the number one commodity for the Elitist Class and they don't even know it. They are exploited by The Elitist Class that would have no credibility with the people outside the fraternity without them. It is interesting to note that the fraternity was founded by 3 undergraduates and the first national offices were held by this Undergrad class yet today they are never even considered to hold the national office of Grand Basileus or any of the major political positions of the fraternity. Aside from not sharing any significant political power with the undergrads, the Elitist Class shares very little of the fraternity's revenue with this class and this class has no control over fraternity's internal economy. This class fights within itself over trivial matters yet wages no resistance to the Elitist Class that exploits it. Nor does it raise any significant resistance against any external forces opposed to its people in general. However, it is able to generate some revenue on entertainment venues but it is poorly managed and is never used collectively to gain collective economic strength to increase political power and spread true friendship by the uplift of the masses.

If this Class can figure out the exploitative strategy of the Elitist and Petty Bourgeoisie within the Class Struggle, they have the most potential of any of the aforementioned classes for starting the revolution for transformative change in the fraternity. This class must begin to understand that they are "the production" for the Elite just as "the wage worker" or slave is for the corporate ruling class. They are taxed by an Elitist Class which does not value friendship and continues to loot fraternity coffers for their personal private interest. Once this is internalized in their conscience, hopefully their anger from being ostracized, unduly expelled, coupled with being exploited, will prompt them to start an intra- fraternal socialist revolution. That intra-fraternal Socialist Revolution would allow them to utilize the fruits of their labor and production for the collective good of all.

This book is written by and for the Revolutionary Owt Undergraduate/Proletariat Class and the community it must more effectively serve. Hopefully, it inspires "Revolution" with no fear or apology for using the term. It is also a hope that the reader will see that the class struggle within Omega is a pervasive class struggle that can be transformed through, but not limited to, the ideas aligned with the principles of collective work, responsibility and cooperative economics presented in this book. Transformative change is what will be necessary for true uplift. We are convinced that this is our best egalitarian option. If we happen to be misunderstood in this book it is perhaps because of our global miseducation. But if there is any faith or trust in our fraternity, please read all of these words, understand them, study them, and ask questions about them because they are important to our existence as a fraternity and as a people. Forgive the imperfections in these ideas and work to perfect the imperfections. We expose the Elitist's exploitative schemes in order to awaken the "Owt" Class. And we proudly agitate for the Unduly Expelled, Ostracized and Disenfranchised brothers. We are the embodiment of a socialist movement in our fraternity and we would love to see these ideas permeate through all black organizations. Being an Outcast for so long forced some of us to have to understand our status in order to change it. That required reading the Omega history, law, finance and the conditions of the expelled brothers of Omega. It also required learning macro geopolitics in order to better understand intra-fraternal politics. We are prepared for the task of transformative change and the ideas of this book must inspire us to transform the class struggle into a struggle for cooperative economic and collective work and responsibility.

Chapter 4

Omega's Celebrity Drive – The Last Joy Ride to Death or The Marketing Mule for the Movement

As discussed in the previous chapter regarding the class struggle within Omega, the Owt Undergrad/Proletariat Class is the life blood of the fraternity and it attracts people of all walks of life seeking to be a part of Omega. The enthusiasm and mystique of Omega is carried by this class of brothers due to their endurance through the challenging ritualistic process of which they go through as well as the special character they had to have had inside to complete the process. That mystique has attracted major media personalities to join Omega after witnessing brothers from the Owt Undergrad/Proletariat Class on their various undergraduate campuses or military bases nationally/internationally. This chapter provides some ideas as to how the major media personalities/celebrities could play a major role in marketing and financing Omega's movement toward revolutionary relevance. It will also provide some critical analysis as to how a drive for celebrity recruitment is not only inconsistent with Omega but has the potential to devalue the quality of Omega. One of Omega's earliest Brothers, Walter H. Mazyck, posted a letter in 1925 in Omega's national publication called "The Oracle". The letter was entitled, "Members vs. Men". In that letter, Brother Mazyck warns Omega Psi Phi, Inc. not to enter the race for recruiting members just for the sake of increasing membership as he had begun to witness amongst other fraternities. He called for Omega to maintain high standards and to continue to develop Omega Psi Phi, Inc. to be a fraternity that fostered real and substantive brotherhood through making Omega the most challenging fraternity to enter. Walter H. Mazyck's letter is relevant to this chapter because if Omega continues to enter the race to recruit celebrities rather than continuing to develop Omega into a fraternity that makes the men with the highest potential to become celebrities, it could lead to our last joy ride to death. We have equated these ill-advised actions as the "Joy Ride to Death" because a joy ride is thrilling but aimlessly reckless and often leads to a collision. Many of the Elitist Class brothers that have engaged in these actions are often thrilled to death at the idea of a 'so called' celebrity being given the sacred yoke of Omega so that they can gain a temporary piece of that celebrity. However, to sell Omega for a piece of temporary celebrity status is aimless, reckless and on a collision course metaphorically destine to be struck by a star in the midst of their 'star struck" escapades. Now that's a Joy Ride to death.

Walter H. Mazyck's letter has been posted in entirety below:

Members versus Men

"The Greek Letter Societies among our group appear to have entered into a period of mad competition for obtaining members. Scarcely a student on the college campus but wears a pledge pin or a fraternity pin. Are the fraternities forgetting their original high standards? Can it be said that every man who enters college is of Fraternity material? If in any place, Omega has entered this mad race for members, pause and consider.
The value of our Fraternity is not in numbers, but in men, in real brotherhood. Eight men thoroughly immersed in the true Omega

spirit are far greater assets than eighty with lukewarm enthusiasm. If any chapter has reached the maximum in numbers for efficient work and brotherly cooperation, let it initiate each year only a number of men equal to those leaving the chapter by way of graduation or otherwise.
Men, real men of Omega caliber, strive for that which is most difficult of attainment. Keep Omega the most difficult Greek letter Society in which to obtain membership and be assured that Omega material will never be found lacking."

Prior to this chapter, a chapter was devoted to the class struggle occurring in Omega today. As an addendum to that chapter it is necessary to shed some light as to how Omega's celebrities and honorary brothers fit into that class struggle and their potential impact on past, present and future Black Fraternal Relevance to the Global African Struggle.

There are many celebrity brothers that have gone throw the ritualistic process and became nationally/internationally famous within their particular area of expertise after completing the process. These brothers utilize the tenants learned through their ritualistic process to endure the challenges leading to their ultimate success in their various fields. They remain –for the most part – committed to Omega culturally and emotionally but are often not politically or economically attached largely because the ritualistic process does not typically place enough focus on the economics and politics of the fraternity. However, it is likely that if Omega was to organize and educate toward economic self-determinations in a viable way, these brothers would be willing to support those efforts due to their undying cultural and emotional tie. These type of brothers may lead to the portion of the title of this chapter called "Omega's Celebrity Drive – The Marketing Mule for the Movement". They possess this potential because they often maintain the cultural and emotional attachment that leads to enthusiasm for the fraternity which is inevitably noticed by the masses of people due to their celebrity status. This in turn results in free marketing for Omega as well as potential capital investment. If Omega decides to take the necessary steps for self –determination outlined in this book, the celebrity marketing has the potential to bring more people to the movement as supporters, external/internal benefactors and members.

However, in discussing the class of anybody in American, you cannot avoid the conversation of the American miseducation that guides ones thoughts and actions no matter what organization they belong. With that said, there are celebrity brothers that have been educated in a manner that understands the Global plight of African people and the actions that will be necessary to forward that struggle. This class of celebrity brothers is few and far between but they do exist and they have played and play a critical role in furthering the struggle of oppressed people. That is Omega's purpose and it is the hope of literature such as this to bring those brothers together so that their individual efforts can be combined to a collective Omega effort that serves to uplift the downtrodden.

There are other brothers of this type of celebrity class that completed the ritualistic process that may not have received the Afrocentric geopolitical education that would guide their actions toward contributing to a culturally and economically relevant Omega. But they often maintain the true spirit of brotherhood and with proper explanation and education from the brothers that have received an Afrocentric geopolitical education, they still possess the potential to be the marketing mules for the movement.

There are many celebrities that do not go through a complete ritualistic process but do go through a less challenging process and pay a fee to be a part of Omega. There are others that may have actually gone through a ritualistic process but did not complete the process for reasons that may not have been in their control or they may not have had the endurance necessary to complete the process. These type of celebrity brothers have the potential to lead the portion of the title of this chapter called "Omega's Celebrity Drive – The Marketing Mule for the Movement" or some could take Omega into the direction of "The Last Joy Ride to Death". Sometimes such celebrity class of brothers are so enthused about being a part of Omega, they show the world their enthusiasm for Omega every time they get a chance. However, this enthusiasm wanes for those not as emotionally attached and the reduced emotional attachment is often due to them not having to earn Omega through enduring the ritualistic process. The enthusiasm wanes partly due to the inundation of opportunistic brothers attempting to exploit celebrity brothers for their own personal gain. In any case and for various reasons, as a celebrity, the public naturally sees the lack of enthusiasm and it can affect public opinion of Omega. Additionally, because celebrity brothers are in the public eye, it makes Omega vulnerable to any derogatory or false statements these brothers make about Omega as well as any unbecoming public behavior celebrity brothers may exhibit. That risk of vulnerability can be caused by any brother within the class struggle spectrum but it may be amplified by celebrity brothers that are not as emotionally attached to Omega and don't understand the necessary discretion involved in representing Omega. This vulnerability could lead to Omega's "Last Joy Ride to Death" because while Omega's leadership increases its recruitment of celebrities for the sake of enlisting celebrities, it increases its vulnerability to negative marketing by celebrity brothers that are not emotionally attached or truly committed to its development. So while at first the brothers have a proverbial 'joy ride' by hanging with celebrities and watching them pseudo-represent Omega through mass media, that Joy ride can turn deadly to Omega's image very quickly as a result negative publicity and accumulating brothers with limited enthusiasm.

Additionally, the level of Afrocentric geopolitical education and understanding of this class of celebrity brothers will also play a critical role as to whether they will support Omega's movement for economic self-determination in order to become relevant to the global African struggle. If they have poor education they may not only decline support of such movements, but publicly mock them and contribute to the death of such movement. If they have a rich geopolitical understanding, they will not only support through media promotion but through finance, education and actions.

There are brothers of which Omega selects has honorary brothers based on their extraordinary service to humanity. When these selections are carefully researched, it is an honor for Omega to have these men accept Omega's honor of them. In these cases, Omega has the potential for a positive "Marketing Mule" and as noted above, if they have a rich global pan-African understanding, they will not only support through media but through finance, education and actions.

However, honorary brothers are often selected solely by the Omega Elitist Class. As noted, the Omega Elitist Class are conservative and reactionary brothers so in turn they often select honorary brothers from that global perspective. That can negatively affect any movement for relevance to the global African Struggle. Additionally, the recent leadership of Omega more often offers Honorary Membership because of the person's commercial notoriety and financial status rather than their extraordinary service to humanity.

These types of actions leads to the portion of the title of this chapter called "Omega's Celebrity Drive - The Last Joy Ride to Death". But if we want Honorary Members of Celebrity status, to aid us in becoming more relevant to the Global African Struggle, we must begin to not only include the revolutionary class of brothers in the decision process of honorary membership but also offer honorary membership to men that have done extraordinarily relevant work in the Global African struggle. That will provide more honorary brothers as Marketing Mules for the Movement.

Below is a list of some famous Omega media personalities. The readers can decide for themselves where these celebrities may be classified.

- **Rev. Dr. Jeremiah Wright** – Pastor Emeritus Trinity United Church of Christ (TUCC)
- **Kevin Alexander Gray** – Author, Activist, Political Campaign Manager
- **Rev. Jesse Jackson** - Founder of both entities that merged to form Rainbow/PUSH. Candidate for the United States Presidency in 1984 and 1988. Served as "Shadow Senator" for DC from 1991 to 1997.
- **Min. Tony Muhammad** - Western Regional Minister of the Nation of Islam
- **Jessie Hill** - President of Atlanta Life Insurance Company.
- **Earl Graves** - Chairman and CEO of Black Enterprise Magazine.
- **Therman McKenzie** - Former Co-Owner of M & M Products (Sta Soft Fro).
- **Nathaniel Bronner** - Co-Owner of Bronner Brothers Beauty.
- **Grant Reynolds** Major role in desegregating the United States Armed Forces.

- **James Nabrit** - Former Dean of the Howard University Law School and former president of Howard University.
- **Roy Wilkins** - Executive Director of the NAACP.
- **Ernest Green** - Civil Rights Activist - Little Rock 9
- **Benjamin Hooks** Executive Director of the NAACP
- **Wiley Branton** - Attorney of the "Little Rock Nine" and former Dean of Howard University School of Law.
- **Oliver Hill** - Civil Rights attorney. 1999 Presidential Medal of Freedom recipient
- **Dr. Carter G. Woodson** - The earliest and most outspoken proponent for the study of Black History.
- **Benjamin E. Mays** - President Emeritus of Morehouse College, writer and lecturer.
- **Professor Frank Coleman** - Professor and head of the Physics Department, Howard University.

- **Herman Dreer** - Teacher, minister, writer, and author of The History of Omega Psi Phi Fraternity, Inc.
- **William Hastie** - First Governor of the Virgin Islands.
- **Robert C. Weaver** - Former U.S. Secretary of Housing and Urban Development (HUD).
- **Clifford L. Alexander, Jr.** - Secretary, Department of the Army.
- **Lawrence Douglas Wilder** - Former Governor of the Commonwealth of Virginia.
- **Togo West** - Secretary of the Army.
- **James E. "Jim" Clyburn** - The House Majority Whip in the 110th Congress. (2nd Black to hold that position).

- **Vernon E. Jordan, Jr.** - 2001 Springarn Medal recipient. Executive Director of United Negro College Fund and a former president of the National Urban League.
- **Clarence Lightner** - 1st Black Mayor of Raleigh, NC. Held the posts of the Director of the CDC and the Administrator of the Agency for Toxic Substances and Disease Registry from 1993 to 1998.
- **Walter E. Washington** - 1st Home-Rule mayor of the District of Columbia. Former Executive Director of the National Capital Housing Authority.
- **George L.P. Weaver** - Former U.S. Secretary of Labor.
- **Kendrick B. Meek** - Congressman serving the 17th Congressional District of Florida since 2003. A former trooper with the Florida Highway Patrol where he became Florida's 1st African-American to promoted to the rank of Captain.

- **Dr. Ernest Everett Just** - Internationally known biologist and professor at Howard University.
- **Dr. Charles Drew** - Perfected the use of blood plasma; Professor of Surgery at Howard University.
- **Percy Julian** - Discovered the use of foam to extinguish fires and discovered a method of producing cortisone synthetically.
- **Charles Bolden** - Astronaut, graduate of the United States Naval Academy (pilot). NASA Administrator (July 17, 2009 - present).
- **Dr. Ronald E. McNair** - Astronaut, graduate of M.I.T., Ph.D. in Physics
- **Dr. Fred Drew Gregory** - Astronaut, graduate of the United States Air Force Academy (pilot).

- **Dr. Hildrus Poindexter** - Bacteriologist who studied the epidemiology of tropical diseases.

- **Langston Hughes** - poet laureate, playwright, novelist, lyricist, and humorist.
- **Sterling Brown**- Teacher, poet, writer, Professor Emeritus of Literature at Howard University
- **Roland Hayes**- International tenor - 1920's;
- **Max Roach** - Jazz drummer.
- **Bill Cosby** - Comedian, author, and actor.
- **William (Count) Basie**- pianist, composer, arranger, and band leader.
- **Joe Torry** - Comedian, author, actor, and producer.
- **Steve Harvey** - Comedian and actor.
- **Steven A. Smith** – Sports Commentator
- **Rickey Smiley** - Comedian and actor.
- **Tom Joyner** - Radio show host.
- **William DeHart Hubbard** - Sprinter; first black person to represent the U.S.in the Olympic Games
- **Joe Black** - All-time great Brooklyn Dodger baseball pitcher. Lowest ERA in the Major Leagues in 1952.
- **Ed "Too Tall" Jones** – Professional Football
- **Michael Jordan** Professional Basketball
- **Rodger Kingdom** – Olympic Gold Medalist in Track
- **Mo Vaughn** – Professional Baseball
- **Greg Pruit** - Professional Football
- **Irving Fryar** - Professional Football
- **Steve McNair** – Professional Football
- **Jerry Ball** - Professional Football
- **Vince Carter** – Professional Basketball

- **John Sally** – Professional Basketball
- **Corliss Williams** - Professional Football
- **Mark Duper** - Professional Football
- **Clarence E. "Big House" Gaines** - Hall of Fame Basketball coach. Winston-Salem State University from 1946 - 1993.
- **Dr. Edwin Bancroft (E.B.) Henderson** – Captain of Washington 12th Streeters (1906-1910). Known as the "Father of Black Sport History". First Black male to become certified to teach Physical Education in public schools.
- **Keith Jackson** -Professional Football
- **Cedric "Cornbread" Maxwell** - Professional Basketball
- **Shaquille O'Neal** Professional Basketball
- **Brice Taylor** - Football 1920's All-American.
- **Terrence Trammell** - 2-time Olympic silver medalist in 110m hurdles.
- **Charlie Ward** – Professional Basketball Player

Chapter 5

Need for Movement to address Unemployment Crisis through the Development of International Trade Unions

The Capitalist system has three main sources of income consisting of profit, wages and rent (income through controlled natural resources)

As the profit baring, rent controlling capitalist have utilized their capital to control the politics of democratic political systems, the democratic systems have been forcefully influenced to develop policies that decrease the wages of U.S. workers and eliminate wage earning positions in the U.S. – replacing them with lower wage earning positions in other nations with limited to no labor laws or environmental protection laws. Additionally, these profit baring and rent controlling capitalists have lobbied democratically elected politicians to export equipment to manufacture goods and extract natural resources and import extracted resources and manufactured goods to the U.S. with limited tariffs. Meanwhile our nation's poor and oppressed youth are sent over to foreign lands utilizing taxes from the working class to engage in unjust wars to destabilize nations in order to strip them of their natural resources or exploit their cheap labor for the corporate capitalist to profit and control. The Great Revolutionary thinker Don Freeman, has equated the exploitation of our youth as soldiers for U.S. corporate interest as none other than hired mercenary killers. I will go further to say they are exploited as hired mercenary killers with no stock options in the corporation of which they are truly working.

Ironically, there has been no mention of increasing tariffs on U.S. offshore corporations' imports as a means to decreasing the U.S. debt. In contrast, there has been heightened efforts to increase taxes for wage earners and cut social programs which benefit wage earners- including soldiers- and keep their communities safe. The 'Red herring' in this paradox is that U.S. corporations are allowed to move their headquarters offshore and claim greater than 50% of their corporate holdings belong to their purported foreign investors so that they can avoid paying U.S. corporate taxes. Therefore, they contribute minimally to the U.S. tax base that funds the military that makes it possible for them to maintain their corporations in foreign governments. All while the poor and working class soldiers from the U.S. receive no financial benefit from protecting these corporate tax dodgers and it is devastating to the poor people displaced in the nations of which the U.S. military attacks for corporate interest. This is why the late Martin Luther King termed "War" as "An Enemy of the Poor".

The way to address this matter - and in wake of the Trans Pacific Partnership (TTP) - is for the masses of people to build a mass movement utilizing our democratic system to pressure congress and our president to approve legislation to establish the following international laws:

1. Prohibit goods from being sold in the U.S. unless the nations developing the goods follow comparable labor/wage worker laws and environmental laws equal to or better than those in the U.S.

2. U.S. companies operating in foreign lands must at least acknowledge U.S. Labor Union Rights and environmental laws for all employees (foreign and domestic).

3. U.S. Corporations operating abroad must set aside jobs for U.S. citizens to work for U.S. Corporations abroad and for the displaced people of those foreign governments to be offered living wages and workers' rights.

4. U.S. foreign policy should support the establishment of international trade unions by global wage workers to ensure that wages are balanced with those of U.S. and European countries and to ensure that U.S. Corporations are not allowed to violate environmental laws of which they are held accountable for in the U.S.

Case in point, Nigeria is the thirteenth largest oil producing nation in the world and ranks approximately third in its production of "sweet crude" oil in the world. The Niger Delta of Nigeria has been ravaged by U.S. and European Oil Developers. The Niger Delta, is a vast area of approximately 100,000 square kilometers of swamps and creeks where the Niger River washes out into the Atlantic Ocean. The air quality and drinking water has been so harshly polluted that

42

the people of Nigeria are developing numerous environment related chronic illnesses and the average life expectancy is currently 47 years of age. Meanwhile- U.S. citizens and European citizens utilize Nigerian oil in much safer environmental conditions and the U.S. and European Corporations established on Nigerian oil provide drastically higher wages and much safer working conditions for their employees in the U.S. and Europe.

As noted above, the Niger Delta is a vast area of swamps and creeks where the Niger River forms an estuary with the Atlantic Ocean. This ecological fact makes international trades unions become a necessity for sustaining a livable ecosystem for the world. Thus, as ALL R Qs drive Omega Psi Phi into this advocacy we will truly live up to the motto of friendship is essential to the soul by being a friend to the world as we look out for the interest of our friends.

Chapter 6

The Need for African & African Diaspora Advocacy

All R Qs recognizes that the key to ultimate uplift of Black People is the global re-unification with Africa. We recognize that this re-unification must be mental, spiritual, political, economic and physical. As our late great historian and brother Carter G. Woodson eloquently expressed in his book entitled, "The Miseducation of the Negro", much of the pathology of black people culminates from their miseducation about their African Identity and heritage. Brother Carter G. Woodson along with other African intellectuals such as Chancellor Williams, Cheikh Anta Diop, J.A. Rogers, Franz Fanon, Marcus Garvey, George Padmore, W.E.B Dubois, C.L.R James, Walter Rodney, Ivan Van Sertima, Asa Hilliard, Molefi Asante, El Hajj Malik El Shabazz, and Gerald Horne provides a Blue Print for Self-Actualization through the study of history relevant to African people in American and the world as well as pre-colonial African Civilization. As a true testament of the impact that Brother Carter G. Woodson's literature had on our founding fathers, they inducted him into Omega Psi Phi as its 7th Honorary Member. That historical action on the part of our Founders speaks volumes of our early commitment to uplift through a higher understanding of our noble African heritage.

The history taught within the U.S. educational system glorifies Europeans and denigrates Africans. This leads to a false sense of superiority on the part of white students and a sense of inferiority amongst black students. Africans in Americans learning through that process become embarrassed of being African. Their image of themselves becomes negative and it becomes easy for them to reject Africa and take on the ways European oppressors. This creates frustration and anger because they strive to be a part of a cultural system designed for them to fail. They also begin to hate themselves without consciously understanding the manifestations of that self-hatred and this leads to pathological behavior along with mental and physical manifestation of disease.

All R Qs' African and African Diaspora Advocacy programs will establish and support national programs to re-educate black people of their rich African culture. Just as our Founding Fathers sought the guidance from their contemporary intellectuals such as Carter G. Woodson, Chancellor Williams and J.A. Rogers, All R Qs will seek the guidance of our contemporary intellectuals such as Maulana Karenga and Molefi Asante whom has eloquently drafted five minimum characteristics essential to an Afrocentric project which includes the following:

(1) An interest in a psychological location,

(2) A commitment to finding the African subject place,

(3) The defense of African cultural elements,

(4) A commitment to lexical refinement, and

(5) A commitment to correct the dislocations in the history of Africa (Asante, *An Afrocentric Manifesto*, Cambridge: Polity Press, 2007, p. 41).

All R Qs will utilize these five characteristic as we develop and support programs.

All R Qs recognizes that as black people learn to accept and love their African existence, then we will become prepared to participate in movements to end the exploitation, degradation and disrespect of Africa on the part of the U.S.A, Europe and their imperialist partner nations. The ALL R Qs African and African Diaspora Advocacy would develop programs addressing the following:

1. Organize action groups to demand that U.S. foreign relations committee push for Debt forgiveness for all African Nations.
2. Organize actions for African and African nations in the diaspora to refinance their loans from the International Monetary Fund and the World Bank with the BRICS bank for less interest.

3. Organize action groups to demand that U.S. foreign relations committee push to honor the Zimbabwe Land Reform Lancaster Agreement of 1979.
4. Establish strong African Congressional Lobbyist to ensure that all legislation regarding Africa complies with the collective African Agenda benefiting Africa and African people in the diaspora
5. Support the election of African Leaders that maintain the integrity and social and political philosophies of African leaders such as Thomas Sankara, Kwame Nkrumah, Patrice Lumumba, Malik Abdul Nasser, Amilcar Cabral, Chris Hani, Sekou Toure, Ahmed Ben Bella and Julius Nyerere
6. Organize action groups to demand that U.S. foreign relations committee stop supporting the invasions of the Democratic Republic of the Congo by U.S. backed forces from Rawanda and Uganda and work to restore the vision of Patrice Lumumba for the Congo.
7. Re-establish a Comprehensive Reparations Bill for U.S. and Europe to compensate Africans in the United States of America and Africans enslaved in Africa, Caribbean, Central, Latin and South America and Europe.
8. Encourage and support to streamlined immigration policies to establish dual citizenship between the U.S., Africa and the Caribbean for African-Americans
9. Devise a development plan to establish a railroad from the South of Africa to the North to enhance interaction between African Nations as well as trade routes and employment exchange between African Nations
10. Work to bring to fruition the United States of Africa with an economic and military system totally independent of the U.S. and Europe
11. Support African Systems of Government that Nationalize their resources for the benefit of the people (see point 4)
12. Pay reparations for the U.S. backed NATO bombings on Libya and the assassination of Col. Muammar Gadhafi. Provide affirmative action in Libya for the displaced and tortured black African migrants in Libya and the ones living in neighboring

countries in exile. Work to restore the socialist system of the Jamahiriya and re-establish their sovereignty

13. End U.S. corporate monopoly on Caribbean, Latin American, Central American and South American commodity crops and natural resources so that these economies can grow with or without reliance on tourism and foreign aid.
14. Work to restore the Lavalas Party and President Jean-Bertrand Aristide or the like as the democratically elected president of Haiti. Additionally, push foreign policies to remove any debts owed to U.S. or Europe.
15. Push for the End all U.S. sanctions on Cuba, return Guantanamo Bay and pay reparations to them.
16. Push to free all black political prisoners in the U.S. and those in exile and pay restitution to them.

These are large goals, but they must be written and casted into our psychology if they are to come to fruition by our next centennial. As "The Creator" and Manhood are our guide, these are the matters of which we must stand for in order to uplift our people moving toward the year 2111. In the African tradition of the Yoruba people, let us call upon the spirit of Ogún and Oshosi (warriors, scouts and hunters, respectively) to open the roads for these goals. Who knows, by the time we reach 2111, we may have reached the self-actualization level of which we no longer feel the need to have an organization of all African men defining itself as a Greek organization.

Chapter 7

Conclusion/Beginning

A cooperative relationship amongst movements is key to sustaining movements. If Omega is to become relevant to the Global African Struggle it must seize the moment to utilize its economic infrastructure to become a global economic and social movement that also works to sustain other relevant social and economic movements to uplift the oppressed. We hope this book has inspired us to encourage Omega to use its banking system to build such movements economically by the principle of cooperative economics. It is also a hope that Omega begins to utilize its intellectual pool of professionals for the purpose of collective work and responsibility to the global African struggle for we stand on the shoulders of that struggle.

We hope that the short essays presented in this book clearly notes Omega's original purpose to uplift downtrodden humanity and how through its internal class struggle it has been side tracked from a collective effort to systemically fulfill that purpose. We also hope that it is clear that Omega's motto of "Friendship is Essential to the Soul" does not place a limit on friendship to the friendships between men of Omega and that friendship must always be expanded to all humanity and the environment that sustains humanity. As we are friends to the world, our global commitment to advancing the global struggle of the downtrodden must be the core of our existence and we must transcend from the internal class struggle confining our best collective effort to systematically address the oppressed conditions of our friends.

One of the essays of this book called for the Omega's support in the development of international trade unions. That action is relevant to uplifting humanity and the environment which sustains humanity because international trade unions have the potential to balance international wages so that multinational corporations would not have the luxury of avoiding environmental laws and depressing international economies to drive wages down internationally in order to move manufacturing out of places with more eco-friendly and humane environmental and labor laws, respectively. This can uplift our environment and humanity while placing Omega at the forefront of leadership amongst any known fraternal order.

The essay regarding African Advocacy would place Omega on the forefront of black fraternal organizations that acknowledge the inherent connection between Africans in Africa and the diaspora. The scholarship of the men of Omega should make this historical fact apparent and move to connect all movements for African people throughout the world as one and the same. Once making this vital self-actualization, we can begin to use our scholarship to impose U.S. legislation for the benefit of all Africans which would most certainly prove to uplift downtrodden humanity. We should also strive to utilize our banking system to collaborate on economic and infrastructure development projects with Africa. Additionally, our scholarship should be used to collaborate on cultural education between all Africans. Lastly, our banking system must collaborate with emerging international banking systems from emerging economies that challenge the western banking system which is largely responsible for our oppression.

Again, Omega is uniquely positioned to be a relevant force in uplifting our oppressed friends. It was designed for that purpose. It has an economic infrastructure with a means of production as well as a means of producing and managing finance capital. It also has an intellectual infrastructure because it possesses some of the best educated men in the United States and has consequently created an African intelligentsia capable of leading in every professional discipline.

All we need now is the vision and the collective will to utilize our resources for cooperative development and good will. If this divine purpose is fulfilled, we will all be uplifted through our Manhood, Scholarship and Perseverance.

www.ingramcontent.com/pod-product-compliance
Lightning Source LLC
Chambersburg PA
CBHW030542290526
45786CB00004B/1824